Being Tolerant

by Jill Lynn Donahue   illustrated by Stacey Previn

PICTURE WINDOW BOOKS
Minneapolis, Minnesota

Special thanks to our advisers for their expertise:

Kay Augustine
National Director and Character Education Specialist, Ignite
West Des Moines, Iowa

Terry Flaherty, Ph.D., Professor of English
Minnesota State University, Mankato

Editor: Shelly Lyons
Designer: Tracy Davies
Page Production: Melissa Kes
Art Director: Nathan Gassman
Associate Managing Editor: Christianne Jones
The illustrations in this book were created with acrylics.

Picture Window Books
5115 Excelsior Boulevard
Suite 232
Minneapolis, MN 55416
877-845-8392
www.picturewindowbooks.com

Printed in the United States of America.

All books published by Picture Window Books
are manufactured with paper containing at least
10 percent post-consumer waste.

Library of Congress Cataloging-in-Publication Data
Donahue, Jill L. (Jill Lynn), 1967-
Being tolerant / by Jill Lynn Donahue ; illustrated by
Stacey Previn.
p. cm. — (Way to be!)
ISBN-13: 978-1-4048-3776-8 (library binding)
ISBN-10: 1-4048-3776-0 (library binding)
1. Toleration—Juvenile literature. 2. Difference
(Psychology)—Juvenile literature. I. Previn, Stacey, ill.
II. Title.
HM1271.D66 2007
179'.9—dc22   2007004570

Being tolerant means being respectful of the differences among people. Tolerant people can be friends with people who are very different from themselves.

There are many ways to be tolerant.

Cassidy is a new student at school. At lunch, Billy and his friends invite her to sit with them.

Billy and his friends are being tolerant.

Gunnar's friends ask him to play a word game. Gunnar is slow at first, but his friends are patient.

Gunnar's friends are being tolerant.

Sam really wants to go outside for recess. But he waits for Joe so they can go together.

Sam is being tolerant.

Maria and Betsy form a club for girls only. Later, Tim asks if he can join their club. The girls change the rules so Tim can join the club.

The girls are being tolerant.

Steve and Carly live with their dad. Kay lives with both of her parents. The families enjoy spending time with each other.

The families are being tolerant.

Some of the boys don't want girls on their baseball team. But Sarah wants to play, so Kyle asks Sarah to join them.

Kyle is being tolerant.

14

15

Miguel's family celebrates Christmas. John's family celebrates Hanukkah. Their families join each other for both of the holidays.

The families are being tolerant.

Tyson has to get glasses. The next day, none of his classmates make fun of his new glasses.

The students are being tolerant.

Cole is having trouble with math. LaVonne helps him with his homework.

LaVonne is being tolerant.

Stan's parents like the mayor. Michael's parents want a new mayor. Stan's and Michael's families are friends.

The families are being tolerant.

To Learn More

At the Library

Headley, Justina Chen. *The Patch*. Watertown, Mass.: Charlesbridge, 2006.

Lamote, Lisa Edman. *Don't Judge a Book by Its Cover*. Rollinsford, N.H.: BookMann Press, 2006.

Miller, Connie Colwell. *Tolerance*. Mankato, Minn.: Capstone Press, 2006.

On the Web

FactHound offers a safe, fun way to find Web sites related to this book.
All of the sites on FactHound have been researched by our staff.

1. Visit www.facthound.com
2. Type in this special code: 1404837760
3. Click on the FETCH IT button.

Your trusty FactHound will fetch the best sites for you!

Index

Look for all of the books in the Way to Be! series:

Being a Good Citizen

Being Brave

Being Considerate

Being Cooperative

Being Courageous

Being Fair

Being Honest

Being Respectful

Being Responsible

Being Tolerant

Being Trustworthy

Caring

Manners at School

Manners at the Table

Manners in Public

Manners in the Library

Manners on the Playground

Manners on the Telephone